Barry Sanders

Barry Sanders
Rocket Running Back

Jack Kavanagh

Lerner Publications Company ▪ Minneapolis

To my grandsons — here are fine footsteps for Peter, Jeffrey, and Kevin Martin to follow.

This book is available in two editions:
Library binding by Lerner Publications Company
Soft cover by First Avenue Editions
241 First Avenue North
Minneapolis, Minnesota 55401

LIBRARY OF CONGRESS CATALOGING-IN-PUBLICATION DATA

Kavanagh, Jack
    Barry Sanders : rocket running back / Jack Kavanagh.
      p.   cm. — (The Achievers)
    Summary: Traces the life of the Detroit Lion running
back from his childhood and college career at Oklahoma
State University to his professional career, religious affil-
iations, and personal interests.
    ISBN 0-8225-0517-7 (lib. bdg.)
    ISBN 0-8225-9635-0 (pbk.)
    1. Sanders, Barry, 1968-   —Juvenile literature. 2. Foot-
ball players—United States—Biography—Juvenile litera-
ture. [1. Sanders, Barry, 1968-   . 2. Football players.
3. Afro-Americans—Biography.] I. Title. II. Series.
GV939.S18K38   1993
796.332'092—dc20
[B]
                                            92-30022
                                            CIP
                                            AC

Manufactured in the United States of America

1 2 3 4 5 6 – P/JR – 99 98 97 96 95 94

Contents

Speed and agility are Barry's most powerful weapons.

1
Crowd Pleaser

Detroit Lion running back Barry Sanders tucked the football under his arm and headed downfield. He swung wide behind his blockers and dashed down the sideline. The Dallas Cowboy tacklers—those his blockers had missed—were left in the dust or side-stepped. Thanks to Barry's amazing speed and his ability to "turn on a dime," he ran into the end zone without a defensive player even laying a hand on him.

On this January day in 1992, Barry was leading the Detroit football team to its first playoff win in more than 30 years. The last time the Lions won a division title, the 23-year-old Sanders had not even been born.

Barry had been playing professional football for just three seasons. He had been named the top player in college football during his junior year at Oklahoma State University. Now he was earning honors as one of the best players in the National Football League (NFL).

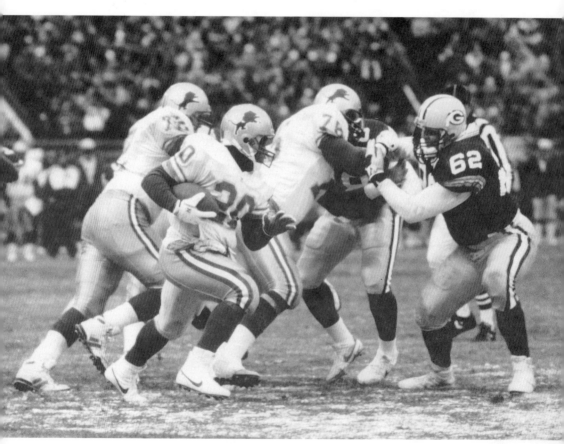

Barry weaves through heavy traffic against Green Bay.

Barry is modest about his achievements.

Barry could catch a pass with one hand or snag the football in a crowd. He could score a touchdown by driving through a pile of defenders or by simply diving over them. But the touchdowns the fans enjoyed most came on Barry's long zigzag jaunts to the goal line. Football fans everywhere roared when the 200-pound Sanders left tacklers 50 or more pounds heavier grabbing in frustration at the space where he had just been.

As Barry ended his game-clinching, 45-yard romp against Dallas, he quietly handed the football to an official. He didn't show off in the end zone by spiking the ball, strutting, or waving his finger. Barry didn't have to tell the world how good he was. The fans, with their cheers, said that Barry Sanders was Number One.

Coaches thought Barry was too small for high school football.
He proved them wrong.

2
Off to a Running Start

William and Shirley Sanders are proud of their 11 children—every one of them. They are especially proud of their youngest son, Barry, the eighth child in the family and a star running back for the Detroit Lions.

No one had counted on Barry finding success as a professional football player. Instead, the Sanders believed that education was the best route to success. Shirley Sanders insisted that all her children study hard in school. Even after Barry was an NFL star, he kept working on his college degree between seasons.

Barry grew up in a crowded, three-bedroom house in the north end of Wichita, Kansas. Shirley Sanders, a nurse, and William Sanders, a roofer, worked long hours to support their family. When bad weather prevented William from working outdoors, he took indoor carpentry jobs. There was no time to waste with 11 children to raise and educate.

Looking back on his childhood, Barry recalls, "We were raised to use what you have and not go around looking for more. We were taught not to be greedy or obsessed with what you couldn't have. It was instilled in us as kids. It's a trait that comes from not having very much outside and a lot inside.

"We worked," Barry says. "Mom had our noses in the books. When they weren't, Dad had us out there doing something." Working with his father—pouring hot tar during sweltering Kansas summers—convinced Barry that studying was better than tarring roofs.

When Barry was a boy, his brother Byron was his closest friend. Byron was born in 1967 and Barry about a year later, on July 16, 1968. Byron and Barry were natural athletes from the start. They played all sports. Basketball and baseball might have lost a future superstar when Barry began to play football at age nine. After Barry scored three touchdowns in a youth-league football game, his father rewarded him with a pair of new football shoes. They were bright red and endorsed by O. J. Simpson, then the greatest running back in the NFL.

With both parents working, Barry and Byron sometimes skipped school and got into mischief on the streets of Wichita. William and Shirley Sanders soon put their sons on the right path, though. The Sanders insisted that their boys attend school, study, and earn passing grades if they wanted to play team sports.

Weighing less than 150 pounds, Barry was considered small for high school football. But William Sanders saw greatness in Barry before others did.

Barry also excelled at basketball as a teenager.

William persuaded the football coaches at Wichita's North High School to put Barry in the lineup. As a junior, he caught passes as a wide receiver and ran back kicks.

His brother Byron, playing tailback, was the team's star ballcarrier. Bigger and heavier than Barry, Byron went to Northwestern University in Illinois on a football scholarship.

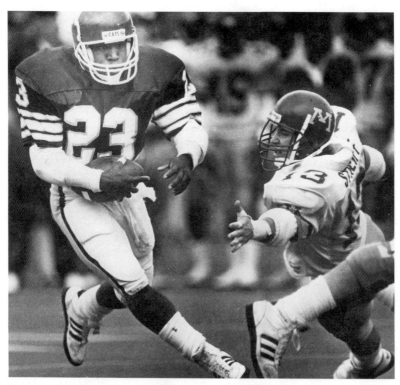

Byron Sanders was All-Big Ten as a tailback for Northwestern and was drafted by the Chicago Bears in 1989.

Even as a senior, Barry did not make North's starting lineup right away. Coach Dale Burkholder was afraid the undersized player would get hurt. In addition, Burkholder did not like Barry's way of running the ball. The shortest distance to the end zone was a straight line, the coach said. He thought Barry "juked" too much—moving from side to side to avoid tacklers.

Finally, William Sanders demanded more playing time for his son. If Barry was to follow Byron to college, only a football scholarship would get him there. Even with William holding two jobs and Shirley working at a hospital, the Sanders didn't have enough money to pay college tuition for everyone.

With only six games left on the 1985 schedule, Barry finally started for North High at tailback. In his first game, he ran the ball 274 yards and scored four touchdowns. He earned the starting running back job and rushed for almost 1,400 yards for the rest of the season. He averaged 10.3 yards per carry.

Despite averaging six touchdowns a game, Barry had emerged as a high school star almost too late. Wichita is in the heart of the Big Eight Conference—a sports league made up of state colleges in Kansas, Nebraska, Oklahoma, Missouri, Iowa, and Colorado. The conference schools decide early in the season which high school players will get scholarships. The University of Nebraska and the University of Oklahoma, the most powerful teams in the Big Eight, overlooked Barry. The only major college that showed any interest was Oklahoma State University.

The Oklahoma State Cowboys already had a great running back, Thurman Thomas. But the OSU coaching staff thought Barry might fit in as a backup for Thomas and as a kick returner. Oklahoma State offered Barry a scholarship to attend school and play football.

Barry Sanders quietly slipped onto the OSU campus in Stillwater, Oklahoma, with the incoming freshmen in 1986. The coaches didn't expect much of Barry. They assigned him to special teams (the punt and kickoff return units) because he was fast. Thurman Thomas, already an All-American as a sophomore, was OSU's reigning star. Barry Sanders played his freshman and sophomore seasons in the big shadow Thomas cast across the OSU campus.

Barry liked college life. He fit in easily with the other young people in his dormitory. But at first, the other students weren't sure if Barry Sanders was for real. He spent as much time in the college library as he did in the gym. And he didn't take snap courses either. Barry wanted to use his mind. He worked on a degree in business management. He studied accounting, economics, and statistics.

In the gymnasium, Barry worked at expanding his body. He was 5 feet, 8 inches and would not grow any taller. But he gained weight by building up his muscles. Barry checked in at OSU at 180 pounds. By working out in the weight room, he added more than 20 pounds to his frame.

Barry's legs became particularly strong. He increased his strength until he could squat-lift 556 pounds and bench-press 350. His vertical leap reached 41 inches. That's Michael Jordan's stratosphere!

Barry did much more than anyone had expected during his first two years at Oklahoma State. He not only backed up Thurman Thomas, he also made the most of his opportunities to run the ball. As a sophomore, he picked up 622 yards on only 111 carries. Three times he gained more than 100 yards in a game.

At Oklahoma State, Barry was serious about football *and* his studies.

Opposing coaches began to tell their defensemen not to hurt Thomas—they were afraid Barry would be sent in as a replacement!

Barry also became well known for returning kicks. He led the National Collegiate Athletic Association (NCAA) in 1987 with an average of 31.3 yards per kickoff return—two were spectacular 100-yard touchdown runs. Barry was second in the nation in punt returns. He averaged 15.2 yards and carried two punts back for touchdowns. He was named to *The Sporting News* College All-America Team as a kick returner.

While Barry was enjoying his sophomore season, rumors began to surface that some high school players had received special deals to play football for OSU. Coaches and alumni had offered players new cars, fancy clothes, money, and easy jobs at good pay, some people said, in exchange for signing on with Oklahoma State.

Barry had no special arrangements, though. He wore jeans and sweaters and drove an eight-year-old Pontiac. During the summer, he bagged groceries at a local supermarket. Barry was happy just to be in school. All he wanted was a chance to play football and to earn a college degree.

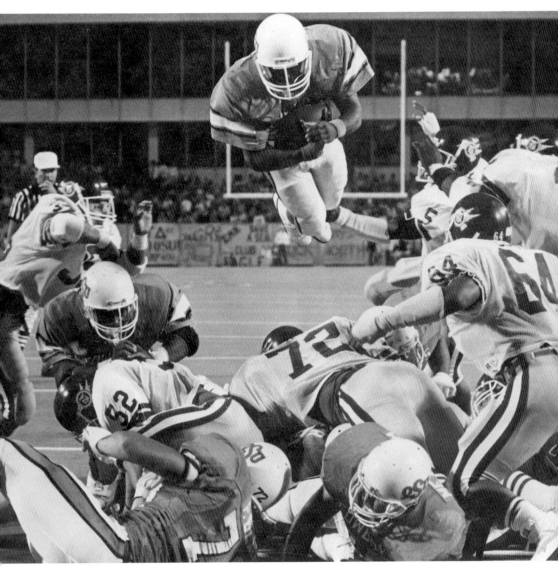

People often compare Barry to Thurman Thomas. Here, Thomas flies into the end zone for an Oklahoma State touchdown.

During his junior year, Barry captured the attention of reporters, fans, and coaches nationwide.

3
Suddenly, Here's Sanders

College football fans simply were not expecting Barry Sanders' 1988 season. True, there had been signs the year before that Barry was something special. Yet the 1988 season was well under way before the media and the fans discovered him.

Oklahoma State helped keep Barry a secret by scheduling its first three football games at night. The university had invested $1 million to light Lewis Field for night games. The lights were a modern touch for the 68-year-old playing field. But night games were not broadcast on national television. Game highlights were not shown on evening news reports, and OSU scores were not even printed in most Sunday newspapers.

Barry and quarter-back Mike Gundy were a tough offensive combination for OSU.

Barry Sanders began the 1988 season against a top-10 team, Texas A&M, by running the opening kickoff back 100 yards for a touchdown (for the second year in a row). But few people outside of Oklahoma heard about the accomplishment.

Barry Sanders' running ability fit right in with the talents of his teammates. Barry worked with quarterback Mike Gundy, a talented passer, and Hart Lee Dykes, one of college football's greatest pass-catchers. Barry ran behind a brawny offensive line of seven seniors who called themselves "the War Pigs." The year before, they had cleared the way for Thurman Thomas. In 1988 the War Pigs took new pride in opening holes for Barry Sanders.

But Oklahoma State's defense was as weak as the offense was strong. This combination resulted in high-scoring games, with OSU's defensive unit giving up a whopping 29.7 points a game during 1988. Of course, every time the Cowboys gave up a touchdown, Barry Sanders and the War Pigs came back on the field. When you give the best runner in the game more chances to carry the ball, a lot of records will be broken.

Oklahoma State University won its first four games in 1988. Barry scored in each of them, racking up 13 touchdowns and 812 yards in all.

In the fifth game, the Cowboys faced the University of Nebraska. The Nebraska Cornhuskers, who were also unbeaten, were a college football powerhouse. While they could not keep Barry Sanders from the end zone, they took advantage of the weak OSU defense and outscored him.

Nebraska scored five touchdowns in the first quarter and led 35-0 before Barry could get the Cowboys on the scoreboard. Although Barry scored four touchdowns, the early Nebraska lead was too much to overcome. Oklahoma State lost 63-42. But the 189 yards Barry gained in the game lifted him over the 1,000-yard mark for the season—with six games left to play.

The Cowboys won their next two games, beating Big Eight Conference rivals Missouri and Kansas State. Barry now had 22 touchdowns. Against Kansas State, he broke an NCAA record by tallying his second 300-yard game.

The University of Oklahoma came next on OSU's schedule. Like the Nebraska Cornhuskers, the Oklahoma Sooners were a national powerhouse year after year. More than 50,000 football fans came to Lewis Field in Stillwater as the state's rival teams played a typical high-scoring contest. Although Barry gained 215 yards in the game—the second-best yardage total ever gained against Oklahoma—the Cowboys lost the lead in the final minutes and lost a tough game, 31-28.

The Cowboys knew they would not be the champions of the Big Eight that year. But Barry's fantastic statistics held the nation's interest. He kept piling up yards and touchdowns. He topped 300 yards in a third game—a 63-24 runaway against Kansas—and increased his touchdown total to 31.

Barry scored five times against Kansas. His fourth touchdown broke the college record for touchdowns in a season. Then Barry pushed the record higher by scoring four times against Iowa State, one touchdown coming on an 80-yard run.

Oklahoma State's final game of the season was played under the roof of the Tokyo Dome in Japan. Japanese sports fans wanted to see American college football, and promoters made arrangements to bring two college teams to Tokyo. About 54,000 Japanese fans came to watch OSU take on Texas Tech, another high-scoring team. Barry scored four touchdowns and had his fourth 300-yard game of the season as the Cowboys safely wrapped up the game, 45-42.

Barry's 1988 statistics were almost too good to believe. He set an astounding 24 NCAA single-season records and led the nation with 39 touchdowns. At the start of the season, sportswriters thought Barry and teammate Gerald Hudson *together* might rack up statistics to equal Thurman Thomas. Barry doubled Thomas' numbers all by himself!

"Sanders just transcends everything in the book for running backs," said Jim Van Valkenburg, director of statistics for the NCAA. "He's in a class by himself. It's the best season any rusher has ever had."

Cowboy head coach, Pat Jones, tried to put Barry's season accomplishments into perspective. "It's like a baseball player hitting 75 home runs, stealing 150 bases, winning 25 games, and driving in 200 runs, all in the same year," Jones said.

The Cowboys had one more game to play. They were invited to take on 11-1 Wyoming, the champions of the Western Athletic Conference, in a post-season game—the Holiday Bowl. The game was played in San Diego, California, on December 30, 1988. Before he trotted off the field at the end of the third quarter, Barry had racked up 5 touchdowns, bringing his total for the year to 44!

But Barry was now faced with a tough decision. Should he leave college football and join the pros? Would the 62-14 wipeout of Wyoming be the last game Barry Sanders would play wearing the orange and black colors of OSU?

4
Barry's Big Decision

Barry Sanders learned in Japan that he had won the Heisman Trophy, the highest honor awarded each year in college football. Counting the Heisman votes had been just a formality. Barry received 559 first-place votes from among 721 ballots cast. Most Heisman winners are seniors; Barry was just a junior. Of the 53 previous Heisman winners, only 8 others had won the trophy during their junior year.

The announcement naming Barry Sanders as the Heisman Trophy winner was made in New York City, where Barry's parents and his brother Byron had gathered for a televised program. The CBS television network arranged for Barry to take part in the program via satellite from Tokyo. But Barry was modest and tried to evade the spotlight. He only agreed to appear on the program when his teammates reminded him that he represented Oklahoma State and that they deserved to be recognized too.

Barry pulls away from an Iowa State defender.

Even so, Barry's remarks were few. He told the television audience that he had not wanted to win the Heisman Trophy. A devout Baptist, Barry explained that earning individual honors conflicted with his religious beliefs.

Barry thought his team deserved just as much praise as he did. "My teammates worked so hard," he explained. "It's just hard to see myself getting a lot of credit and seeing those guys get pushed aside."

Barry's father was not so shy. "I have to pinch myself to make sure I am not dreaming," he said in New York City. "It's hard for me to believe that this boy, my son, who grew up in our house, could receive this great honor."

People soon began to wonder whether Barry would turn professional. He still had a year left to play for OSU. But other college players had been excused from their senior seasons so they could enter the professional draft. If the commissioner of the National Football League approved, Barry could be drafted by a pro team.

The Sanders family was divided about the decision. Barry's father and brothers thought Barry should start a professional career at once. Shirley Sanders placed the highest value on education. She herself returned to school and completed a bachelor's degree at Wichita State University after her children were grown. She wanted Barry to stay in school and graduate with his class. Barry's sisters sided with their mom.

Barry was slow to decide. He did not seem impressed with the big bonus he would be paid just to sign a pro contract. He was more concerned about catching up on his studies. When President George Bush invited Barry to Washington, D.C., for the Inaugural Ball, Barry turned down the invitation. He could not leave campus, he explained. The game in Tokyo and the Holiday Bowl had put him behind in his studies.

But soon some news broke that helped Barry look beyond college. The rumors about OSU making special deals with high school players were true. As punishment for breaking NCAA recruitment rules,

Oklahoma State would not be allowed to appear in televised football games or to play in post-season bowl games. Colleges make a lot of money from televised games, and the restrictions would hurt OSU financially.

Barry believed that the punishment would also hurt his football career. He would rather play 16 games a year as a paid professional than 11 games that no one would see outside the college stadium. If NFL Commissioner Pete Rozelle approved Barry's request, he would turn pro. Barry promised his mother he would earn his college degree between football seasons.

Commissioner Rozelle agreed to let Barry enter the NFL draft a year ahead of his scheduled graduation. The teams with the poorest records take first pick of the college players. The Detroit Lions, who had finished last in their division in 1988, made Barry Sanders their first choice.

Barry had hoped another team would pick him. The Lions featured a "run-and-shoot" offense, which relies on sending the ends and flankers on pass routes; they do not block rushing linemen. Instead of having a blocking back to lead the way, Barry would be on his own.

If Barry was going to play for the Lions, he wanted the best contract possible. Athletes hire lawyers to serve as agents and help negotiate contracts with professional teams. William Sanders knew of several good agents. They were not as well known as some, mostly because they were African American. But Barry's father believed that black agents should represent black players. On his father's advice, Barry Sanders asked lawyers Lamont Smith and David Ware to represent him.

The agents spent months haggling with the Lions' negotiators over the terms of Barry's contract. The start of the 1989 NFL season was coming closer and closer. The players were already working out at training camp in southern California. The team's owners thought Barry would be anxious to settle his contract and start training. But Barry's agents urged him to wait for the best possible deal.

At first Barry wasn't excited about signing on with the Lions.

Barry is small—but he's fast!

5
Rookie Runaway

Barry not only missed training camp in 1989, he also missed the exhibition games played before the start of the regular season. But the terms of Barry's contract made the wait worthwhile. Barry would be paid more money than any non-quarterback ever entering the NFL. Three days before the regular season began, Barry signed a five-year, $5.9 million contract with a $2.1 million signing bonus.

But Barry didn't want a big salary because he was greedy. Barry wanted to give 10 percent of his income to his family's church, the Paradise Baptist Church, in Wichita. Barry's pastor, the Reverend Jim Gray, told his tiny, 150-member congregation about the first donation— $210,000, or 10 percent of Barry's bonus money. Barry would not have mentioned the gift himself. He has quietly sent 10 percent of his salary to the church in Wichita ever since.

The Lions opened the 1989 season at home against the Phoenix Cardinals on September 10. Barry sat on the bench during the first half of the game. Finally, with the Lions behind, he trotted onto the field with 5:36 left in the third quarter. The crowd at the Silverdome in Pontiac, Michigan, cheered. The fans expected wonders and they got them.

On the first play, Barry ripped off an 18-yard run. He carried the ball four times in a row. The last carry was a four-yard touchdown run that pulled the Lions back to tie the score. The Cardinals won the game 16-13, though, with a late field goal.

Losing became a familiar pattern for the Lions during the early season. Coach Wayne Fontes had many rookies on the team, including quarterback Rodney Peete from the University of Southern California (runner-up behind Barry in the 1988 Heisman Trophy voting). While the rookies were gaining experience, the team lost five games in a row.

Barry Sanders was an instant star, however. He scored a touchdown against the New York Giants in the second game, yet made a rookie's mistake in the third. Against the Chicago Bears, a rough-playing team known as the Monsters of the Midway, he forgot to wear his hip pads. Although he ran for 126 yards and scored again, he suffered a hip injury. During an October 1 game with Pittsburgh, a limping Barry Sanders gained only one yard. Rodney Peete was also hurt in the game.

The next week the Lions lost 24-17 to Minnesota. Barry did not score, but he ran for 99 yards and caught two passes for another 30 yards.

Finally, the Lions won a game—narrowly beating the Tampa Bay Buccaneers 17-16. With only 23 seconds remaining, Peete, back in action, ran five yards for the winning touchdown. Barry led the way as a blocking back.

Coach Wayne Fontes (left) and starting quarterback Rodney Peete hoped to breathe new life into Detroit's football team.

Peete searches for a receiver while Barry (front) protects him from pass rushers.

The Lions lost two of their next three games, including a close match with the Green Bay Packers. Barry was now returning kickoffs, something he had not done earlier in the season. He ran two kicks back for 41 yards and racked up 184 yards running from the line of scrimmage. Yet Green Bay won 23-20 on a field goal in overtime. The next week, Barry scored twice in another losing contest, this one at Houston by a score of 35-31.

When the Lions went up against Green Bay again, they were looking for revenge. The defensive team created several turnovers early in the game, and Detroit took a 24-3 lead by halftime. The Packers stormed back and trailed only 24-20 by the fourth quarter.

Then Barry went to work. He rushed five times for 21 yards on a scoring drive. But his catch of a 20-yard pass from Rodney Peete saved the game. The ball was thrown too high and behind him. But Barry turned, leaped, and pulled the ball down with one hand. He raced to the five-yard line. Two plays later, Barry dove into the end zone for the final touchdown.

Although the Lions lost the next game to Cincinnati, 41-7 (with Barry scoring his team's only touchdown), they began a winning streak on Thanksgiving Day. The holiday football game is traditional in Detroit. Football fans look forward to the game as much as they do their turkey dinners.

The Cleveland Browns came to Detroit on Thanksgiving and played a hard game. Barry Sanders did not score, but he hauled down two passes for 44 yards and ran for 145. He now led the NFL in yards gained and was the first runner to top 1,000 yards for the season. The Lions won the game 13-10.

On December 3, 1989, Barry scored a touchdown in a 21-14 win over the New Orleans Saints. The next week, the Lions took revenge on the Chicago Bears, who had beaten up on them earlier in the season. This time Barry wore his hip pads and churned his way to two touchdowns—one on an 18-yard run. He picked up 120 yards running and added 59 more on two kickoff returns. He caught three passes for 29 yards. The Lions stunned the crowd at Soldier's Field by beating the Bears 27-17.

The Tampa Bay Buccaneers were easy pickings the next week back at the Silverdome. The Lions beat Tampa Bay for the second time, with a score of 33-7. Barry scored once and again topped 100 yards for the game.

The Detroit Lions, who had started the year by losing their first five games, completed the season with a fifth straight victory—a 31-24 romp over the Atlanta Falcons. Barry had his highest scoring game of the year with three touchdown runs. Detroit had brought its season record from 2-9 to a respectable 7-9.

Barry led the National Football Conference (NFC) running backs with 1,470 yards gained in 1989. Christian Okoye of the Kansas City Chiefs in the American Football Conference (AFC) had gained 10 yards more. Okoye won the overall NFL title. But he had carried the ball 90 more times than Barry, who had missed more than nine quarters during the 1989 season.

Barry could have won the rushing title. But he chose not to! In the final minute of the last game of the 1989 season, with Detroit leading the Atlanta Falcons 31-24, Coach Fontes took Barry aside. "You're 10 yards from leading the league in rushing," Fontes said. "Do you want to go in?"

To the coach's surprise, Barry said no. He told the coach to send in fullback Tony Paige. Paige hadn't carried the ball much that season. Barry didn't care about his own statistics, he wanted to give his teammate a chance to play.

Besides, the Lions had the game sewn up. Why embarrass the opponents just to win a personal title? "When everyone is out for statistics—you know, individual fulfillment," Barry explained, "that's when trouble starts."

The Detroit Lions were still far from being a Super Bowl team. But Barry Sanders received his share of national recognition. He was the only rookie named to *The Sporting News* All-Pro Team in 1989. He was also named Offensive Rookie of the Year by the Associated Press. In winning the honor, Barry received 69 of 70 votes cast by sportswriters and broadcasters who cover the National Football League. True to form, Barry thanked his teammates for helping him win the award. He handed each offensive lineman a gift— a $10,000 Rolex watch—before the final game of the season.

Christian Okoye edged out Barry for the NFL rushing title in 1989.

Barry was also named to play in the NFL's Pro Bowl game—a rare opportunity for a rookie. He led all rushers in the game with 41 yards on 13 carries. He also caught three passes for 23 yards. Then, having proved that his father was right about the decision to turn pro, Barry made good on his promise to his mother by going back to college.

6
Running on High

Barry Sanders hurried back to Michigan after the Pro Bowl game. He now lived in Rochester, a Detroit suburb near the Pontiac Silverdome, where the Lions played and practiced. Barry enrolled at Oakland University, which is located about 10 miles from the stadium. When Barry was not headed toward the Silverdome, he was usually on his way to school.

Barry's football schedule allowed him to take classes during spring semesters only. Playing in the Pro Bowl also kept him from starting his courses on time. In the spring of 1990, Barry slid into a seat in the back of a university lecture hall and quietly began to take notes. Several weeks passed before anyone realized that the studious young latecomer was Barry Sanders.

Coach Fontes hoped his team would carry the momentum of the late 1989 season into the following fall. But although the Lions played more consistently in 1990, they lost more than they had the year before and finished with a 6-10 record.

The Lions were actually better than their record indicated, though. Many losses came in close games—two in overtime and two by just a field goal.

Yet even with a losing team, Detroit fans were beginning to fill the Silverdome. The Lions had not made the playoffs for more than a quarter of a century. With each losing season the Detroit crowds had become smaller. But now Barry Sanders was becoming an attraction. Before he joined the Lions, the average game attendance was about 37,000. With Barry, the team drew nearly 65,000 fans to each game.

The press watched closely as the 1989 Rookie of the Year played his second season. Many second-year players aren't as good as they were the year before. But Barry was even better. By season's end, Barry had gained 1,304 yards on 255 carries and had won the NFL rushing title. He was the first Detroit Lion to win the title since Byron "Whizzer" White in 1940.

Opposing teams had tried to slow Barry down. They put six or seven players on the defensive line, discouraging the run and inviting the Lions to throw more passes. As a result, Barry carried the ball 25 fewer times than he had the year before.

As the Lions improved, more and more Detroit fans flocked to the Silverdome.

But because Barry was not running as often (and he no longer ran back kicks), he increased his role as a pass receiver. In 1989 he had caught 24 passes. In 1990 he snared 35 and turned 3 into touchdowns. He improved his touchdown count from 14 to 16 for the season. The 35 catches also added 462 yards to his total yards gained.

As Barry's fame grew, friends were both impressed and puzzled by his modesty. Barry became uncomfortable when people compared him with great runners of the past. "The Bible suggests it's not [good] for you to...toot your own horn," he explained. Yet the praise continued.

"Barry is better than I was," said Walter Payton, the former Chicago Bear star who gained more yards rushing than anyone in NFL history. "I was never that good."

Barry was named to every All-Pro team that year, and he played in his second Pro Bowl. As soon as the game was over, Barry headed back to Oakland University.

The young business administration major got some firsthand investment experience that semester. When a big supermarket chain announced that the only grocery store in Barry's old neighborhood in Wichita would be closed, Barry bought the store!

Many older people shopped at the neighborhood store because it was within walking distance of their homes. The supermarket also provided jobs for teenagers; Barry himself had worked in the store bagging groceries. Now, Barry's young relatives and neighbors would still be able to find work there. The investment appealed to Barry Sanders.

7
Playoff Payoff

Barry Sanders started his third NFL season with a new contract. People who didn't know Barry might have thought the new agreement gave him more money. But Barry didn't want more money. Barry wanted the blockers who cleared the way for him to be rewarded for their work. The new contract said that the Lions' offensive linemen would each receive an extra $10,000 during any season in which Barry ran for more than 1,000 yards.

The contract also guaranteed Barry a salary for four years—even if he were injured and could no longer play football. Professional football is very dangerous. A player's career can end at any time due to injury.

Barry might have had a hunch about possible injuries when he signed the new contract. His ribs had been badly bruised in pre-season games, and he could not play in the opening game of the regular NFL season against the Washington Redskins.

The Lions had never won a game in Washington. And without Barry in the lineup, they lost to the Redskins for the 15th time. The score was 45-0. Such a humiliating loss would have ruined the season for many teams. Instead, the Lions roared back and ripped off five straight victories.

In his first game back in the lineup, Barry scored a touchdown, as Detroit beat Green Bay 23-14 at the Silverdome. The following week, even though he didn't score, Barry was named NFL Player of the Week for his efforts against the Miami Dolphins. With two minutes to play, Barry made a decisive first down that preserved a 17-13 lead. He gained 143 yards during the game and carried the ball a workhorse 32 times.

The high-scoring Lions rolled on. They beat the Indianapolis Colts 33-24 and defeated Tampa Bay 31-3, with Barry scoring three touchdowns. No one expected the Lions to be so good. Sportswriters commented that Detroit seemed to be winning "on emotion."

A game against Dallas on October 20 showed how an underdog could become a winner. The favored Cowboys stacked the defense against runs and held Barry to just 55 yards. They smothered the passer,

Rodney Peete, and he left the game with a season-ending leg injury.

But the Lions' backup quarterback, Erik Kramer, was a surprise star. When opponents ganged up to stop Barry from running, Kramer came through with the pass. Although the Cowboys outgained the Lions on offense, they lost the ball four times on turnovers. The final score was Detroit 34, Dallas 10.

A tackler tries to rip the football from Barry's hands.

The Lions lost the next two games on the road against Chicago and Tampa Bay, and sports fans started to notice a pattern. The Lions were winning most of their games at home—on artificial turf—in the enclosed Silverdome. Even when Detroit won on the road, the victories usually came against teams that also played in domed stadiums. Was it just a coincidence, or did the Lions have a problem playing on grass?

The losses were followed by a tragic accident, the sort that caused Barry Sanders to insist upon a guaranteed contract that year. During a November 17 game against the Los Angeles Rams, offensive guard Mike Utley was blocking to protect passer Erik Kramer. When the play ended, Utley lay on the ground. He had to be carried off the field on a stretcher.

As Utley went past his teammates, the hushed crowd in the stands saw him give the "thumbs-up" sign to assure everyone that he would be okay. He was wrong. Utley had suffered a career-ending spinal injury that paralyzed him from the chest down.

The thumbs-up gesture became Detroit's symbol for the rest of the season. Drawing upon Mike Utley's bravery, the Lions encouraged each other with a thumbs-up sign when they needed an extra effort. The tribute to their injured teammate gave the emotionally charged Lions the added drive they needed to reach the playoffs and the division championship game.

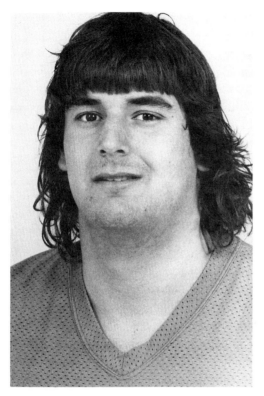

Mike Utley (left) and
Erik Kramer were the
heroes of the 1991
season.

Detroit faced Dallas for the division title. Although
the Lions had won the first matchup that season, the
Cowboys had played better statistically. Dallas had
won 11 of its last 14 games and had beaten the
Chicago Bears in the first round of the playoffs.
Cowboy running back Emmitt Smith had even outgained Barry Sanders.

The Cowboys never had a chance. They stacked
their defense against Barry's running attack, so Erik

Kramer passed instead. Kramer's game was as great as any ever enjoyed by the legendary quarterbacks of the NFL. The run-and-shoot offense worked just the way it was designed in the playbook. Dallas was weak at the cornerback positions, and Kramer kept hitting his receivers for first downs.

The game was already safely in hand before Barry scored on a spectacular 45-yard touchdown run. The play began with Barry carrying the ball on a sweep. The linemen cleared the way for what looked like a short gain. Then Barry spun out of a pile of players and veered away. He burst past the Cowboys' remaining tacklers and zoomed into the end zone.

The final score was 38-6. The Detroit Lions had won their first playoff game in 35 years. They were champions of the NFC's Central Division.

One barrier stood between the Lions and the Super Bowl. They had to beat the powerful Washington Redskins, the Eastern Division winners. Worse, the game would be played at RFK Stadium in Washington, where the season had started with a 45-0 loss. The Lions would be playing outdoors—on grass—in a city where they had never won a game.

Even with Barry Sanders in the lineup, Detroit didn't have much of a chance. Washington's defense was so good that the players could gang up on Barry's runs and still drop back to cover passes. When Detroit fell behind early, the Lions abandoned the running game. Barry even tried to protect passer Erik Kramer by blocking. But Barry Sanders was no match for men 50 and 60 pounds heavier than him. The final score was 41-10.

The Lions wouldn't be appearing in the Super Bowl. Yet few fans were unhappy with the team's performance that season. The Lions had had only 10 winning seasons and had appeared in just three playoff games since 1957. The 12 victories posted in 1991 were a team record.

Barry had scored 17 touchdowns in 1991, the most in the NFL. He led the league in points scored as a runner with 102 and led the NFC in total yards with 1,855. After the 1991 season, Barry Sanders was once again named to the Pro Bowl and *The Sporting News* NFL All-Pro Team. He won the Maxwell Award as the league's Player of the Year and was named Most Valuable Player by the NFL Players Association.

Barry lost the rushing title to Emmitt Smith of Dallas though. With 23 more carries, Smith had 1,563 yards to Barry's 1,548.

The 1992 season was a disappointment, with the Lions winning just three games. Nevertheless, Barry finished a fourth season with more than 1,000 yards gained and increased his career total to 5,674 yards. He played in his fourth Pro Bowl and was named to the popular All-Madden Team, made up of the NFL's hardest working players.

Barry rests on the sideline — but keeps close watch on the action.

Back at Oakland University, Barry is just another student. His classmates say he is open and friendly. He enjoys talking with friends and dating—although he doesn't have one special girlfriend.

Barry is very active in Champions for Christ, a religious organization made up of professional athletes. He believes that his athletic skill is a special gift that God has given him, and that he must use his talents to help others. "I just want to be viewed as a person who believes in God, loves his family, and enjoys being himself," Barry told a *Boy's Life* writer.

On the football field, Barry plays hard and never gives less than 100 percent. But Barry doesn't believe that he alone deserves the cheers. Scoring touchdowns is only important to Barry when the team wins—when everyone can share the victory.

Many people compare Barry to Buffalo Bills running back Thurman Thomas. But Thomas and Sanders are different kinds of runners. Thomas runs over tacklers, while Barry dodges and runs past them. Thomas has made it to the Super Bowl. Barring injuries, Barry Sanders expects to follow the same path. He has already begun a brilliant playing career. Will it lead to an eventual Super Bowl victory? Barry Sanders would be the first to point out that it would be a team victory, the kind he prefers.

BARRY SANDERS' FOOTBALL STATISTICS

Oklahoma State University Cowboys

	Number	Yards	Average	Touchdowns
Rushing				
1986	74	325	4.4	2
1987	111	622	5.6	9
1988	344	2628	7.6	37
Receiving				
1986	0	0	0	0
1987	4	58	14.7	1
1988	19	106	5.6	0
Kickoff returns				
1986	7	166	23.7	0
1987	15	470	31.3	2
1988	21	421	20.0	1
Punt returns				
1986	9	43	4.8	0
1987	18	273	15.2	2
1988	10	94	9.4	1

Detroit Lions

	Number	Yards	Average	Touchdowns
Rushing				
1989	280	1470	5.3	14
1990	255	1304	5.1	13
1991	342	1548	4.5	16
1992	312	1352	4.3	9
Receiving				
1989	24	282	11.8	0
1990	35	462	13.2	3
1991	41	307	7.5	1
1992	29	225	7.8	0
Kickoff returns				
1989	5	118	23.6	0

ACKNOWLEDGMENTS

Photographs reproduced with permission of Mickey Pfleger, pp. 1, 2, 31, 52; Vernon Biever, pp. 6, 8, 32, 36, 47, 56; Detroit Lions, pp. 9, 35, 43, 49; *Wichita Eagle*, pp. 10, 13; Northwestern University, p. 14; Oklahoma State University, pp. 17, 19, 20, 22, 28; Kansas City Chiefs, p. 40; *Detroit Free Press*/Julian Gonzalez, p. 55. Front cover: Tom DiPace; back cover: *Detroit Free Press*/John Stano.